UNDERSTANDING

GLOBAL

WARMING

REBECCA L. JOHNSON

LERNER PUBLICATIONS COMPANY · MINNEAPOLIS

For Earth's young and steadfast guardians

Text copyright © 2009 by Rebecca L. Johnson

Lerner Publications Company
A division of Lerner Publishing Group, Inc.
241 First Avenue North
Minneapolis, MN 55401 U.S.A.

Website address: www.lernerbooks.com

Library of Congress Cataloging-in-Publication Data

Johnson, Rebecca L.
    Understanding global warming / by Rebecca L. Johnson.
      p. cm. — (Saving our living earth)
    Includes bibliographical references and index.
    ISBN 978-0-8225-7561-0 (lib. bdg. : alk. paper)
    I. Global warming. I. Title.
  QC981.8.G56J6454 2009
  363.738'74—dc22   2007048358

Manufactured in the United States of America
1 2 3 4 5 6 — DP — 14 13 12 11 10 09

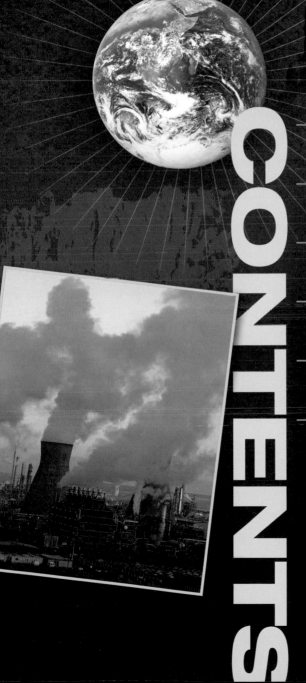

CONTENTS

INTRODUCTION 4

WHAT IS GLOBAL WARMING? 6

TURNING UP THE HEAT 16

EARTH'S CHANGING CLIMATE 24

TACKLING A GLOBAL PROBLEM 40

STRATEGIES FOR A
SUSTAINABLE FUTURE 48

Going Green 58
Glossary 64
Selected Bibliography 66
Further Reading 68
Index 70

INTRODUCTION

Somewhere off the coast of northern Alaska, a polar bear stands on a chunk of sea ice. It is barely bigger than he is. The bear sees a larger, thicker chunk on the horizon. He hesitates. It's a long swim away. But he's desperate for food. The bear lunges into the water and starts paddling.

Polar bears live in the Arctic. This region includes the Arctic Ocean and the cold, treeless land that surrounds it. Seals are polar bears' favorite food. The bears hunt seals from the sea ice that forms on the ocean's surface. The bears crouch at the edge of the ice. They grab seals that come up to the water's surface to breathe.

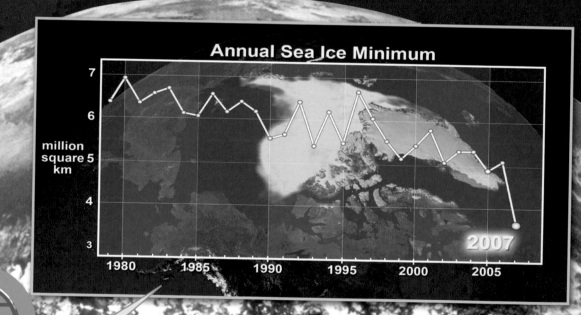

Above: The jagged line in the graph shows the overall decrease in Arctic sea ice since 1979. The background image shows sea ice (white) on the Arctic Ocean during summer 2007. The area covered by sea ice that year was the smallest on record. *Right:* A polar bear stands on a chunk of sea ice in the Arctic Ocean.

In winter, sea ice covers most of the Arctic Ocean. The ice stretches from northern Russia across the North Pole to Canada. When spring arrives, temperatures rise. The sea ice melts back, or retreats, from the land.

Until the late 1980s, the summer sea ice was always close enough to land that polar bears could easily reach it. That's no longer true. Arctic winters aren't as cold as they used to be. Summer temperatures are soaring, melting more and more ice. By midsummer, sea ice retreats as much as 200 miles (322 kilometers) from land.

Some polar bears drown as they try to swim to ice that is too far away. Others starve, unable to catch enough food. If the sea ice keeps shrinking, polar bears may not survive.

Why is this happening? Earth's average surface temperature is increasing. The Arctic is not the only place that's warming. Temperatures everywhere are rising. This worldwide change is called global warming.

Up until the early 2000s, many people doubted that global warming was anything to worry about. But research has erased that doubt. Global warming is changing Earth in ways that spell trouble for polar bears and other living things. It's changing in ways that affect people too. Global warming may be the greatest environmental challenge we've ever faced.

CHAPTER ONE

WHAT IS GLOBAL WARMING?

Yᴏu've probably heard the phrase "global warming" hundreds of times. But what exactly does global warming mean?

Global warming isn't about having a hot day or week or month in one part of the world. It has to do with the average temperature worldwide. Simply put, global warming is the increasing of Earth's average surface temperature over time.

The current warming of Earth began in the mid-1800s. At first it was small and very gradual. But in the 1980s, Earth's average surface temperature began to rise more rapidly. It has been climbing ever since. Eleven of the twelve years from 1995 to 2007 were the hottest on record. Overall, Earth's temperature has risen 1.4°F (0.8°C) since about 1900.

UPS AND DOWNS VS. AVERAGES

Most graphs of recent global temperature show ups and downs. Some years are cooler, and others are hotter. Such differences from year to year are normal. What's more telling is to look at the graph as a whole. That way you see the average trend in temperature. And overall, the trend is up.

SOLAR ENERGY AND HEAT

Why is Earth warming? To answer that question, it's important to understand why Earth is warm in the first place. Think of the last time you were outside in the sun. That sunlight felt warm on your skin, right? Just like your skin, Earth's surface and everything on it is warmed by the sun.

Land, water, and most everything else on Earth absorbs energy from the sun. Earth's average surface temperature has increased rapidly since the 1980s.

The sun constantly radiates, or sends out, enormous amounts of energy. This solar energy travels through space toward Earth. Part of solar energy is visible light. Visible light is solar energy we can see. But we cannot see other parts of solar energy. For instance, infrared radiation (heat) is invisible to our eyes. So is ultraviolet light, which can cause sunburn.

Solar energy passes easily through Earth's atmosphere. Clouds reflect some solar energy back into space. So do snow and ice on the ground. But land, forests, water, and other things on Earth absorb incoming solar energy. And as Earth's surface absorbs solar energy, it warms. The warm surface, in turn, radiates heat.

THE ATMOSPHERE'S LAYERS

Earth's atmosphere is like a blanket of gases around the planet. It has several layers. Each layer blends into the one above it. The lowest layer, closest to Earth's surface, is the troposphere. This is where global warming is occurring. Some changes linked to global warming are also taking place in the stratosphere. That's the next layer up.

THE GREENHOUSE EFFECT

As heat radiates away from Earth's surface, some of it escapes into space. But not all of it. Certain gases in the atmosphere absorb some of the heat before it can escape. Then the gases reradiate that heat toward Earth. They absorb and reradiate heat over and over again. In effect, they trap a certain amount of heat in the atmosphere. Thanks to these heat-trapping gases, Earth's surface and the air just above it stay warm enough for living things to survive.

Scientists call this heat-trapping process the greenhouse effect. That's because Earth's atmosphere works somewhat like the clear covering of a greenhouse.

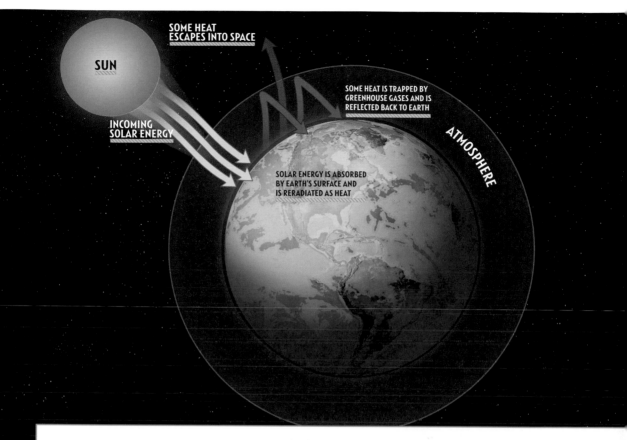

SUN

SOME HEAT ESCAPES INTO SPACE

INCOMING SOLAR ENERGY

SOME HEAT IS TRAPPED BY GREENHOUSE GASES AND IS REFLECTED BACK TO EARTH

ATMOSPHERE

SOLAR ENERGY IS ABSORBED BY EARTH'S SURFACE AND IS RERADIATED AS HEAT

Carbon dioxide and other greenhouse gases in the atmosphere trap some of the heat coming up from Earth's sun-warmed surface. This heat-trapping process is the greenhouse effect.

Sunlight passes through the greenhouse's roof and walls. Solar energy warms the things inside. Then those warm objects radiate heat. But the heat can't travel back out through the glass or plastic. It stays in the greenhouse, raising the temperature inside.

Earth's greenhouse effect is a lot more complicated than what happens inside a greenhouse. What makes Earth's greenhouse effect unique are the heat-trapping gases in the atmosphere. Scientists call them greenhouse gases. And they are the key to global warming.

WATER VAPOR AND CARBON DIOXIDE

What are the atmospheric gases that help keep Earth warm? The two most abundant greenhouse gases are water vapor and carbon dioxide.

Water vapor is water in its gas form. Water vapor gets into the air through evaporation. When water in rivers, lakes, and oceans is warmed by the sun, some is warmed enough to change to water vapor. The water vapor rises into the atmosphere.

Carbon dioxide is a colorless, odorless gas. It is made of one atom of carbon and two atoms of oxygen. Scientists know it as CO_2. Carbon dioxide is not just in the air. It's also in your body. Your cells produce carbon dioxide as a waste product. You get rid of it every time you breathe out. So do lots of other living things. Carbon dioxide is also produced when something burns. It's made when dead plant and animal matter decays (rots) too.

This forest fire is releasing carbon dioxide into the air.

Most living things produce and release carbon dioxide. But plants and algae (plantlike organisms that live in wet places) also take in carbon dioxide. They absorb it from air or water. They use it in a process called photosynthesis. Photosynthesis uses energy from sunlight to change carbon dioxide into food (sugar) for the plants or algae.

THE CARBON CYCLE

Carbon turns up in many kinds of molecules, not just carbon dioxide. In fact, carbon is just about everywhere in the natural world. For example, carbon is in the cells of all living things. The world's oceans contain carbon. Some of it is dissolved in the water. Huge amounts are stored in thick sediments (mud and sand) on the ocean floor. On land,

ATOMS AND MOLECULES

Everything in the world, including gases in the air, is made of molecules. A molecule is the smallest part of a substance that has all the traits of that substance. Molecules are made up of even smaller bits called atoms. A molecule of water includes two atoms of hydrogen (H) and one atom of oxygen (O). So scientists call water H_2O.

Stingrays glide along the ocean floor in the southern Atlantic Ocean. Carbon is stored in the mud and sand on the bottom of the ocean.

carbon is part of every plant leaf and stem. And since dead plants (and animals) often end up becoming part of the soil, soil has a lot of carbon too.

Chances are that the carbon atoms in any given molecule have been a lot of places. They have traveled far and wide over millions of years. That's because carbon moves among living things, the land, the atmosphere, and the oceans in the carbon cycle.

Some carbon moves quickly through the carbon cycle. Imagine lying on thick green grass. Grass blades just inches from your nose absorb carbon dioxide from

Carbon cycles through the natural world in many ways. One way is in molecules of carbon dioxide. Living things, decomposing material, and the burning of fuels all release carbon dioxide. Plants and algae take in carbon dioxide from air and water. The ocean absorbs some atmospheric carbon dioxide. It also releases carbon dioxide back into the air.

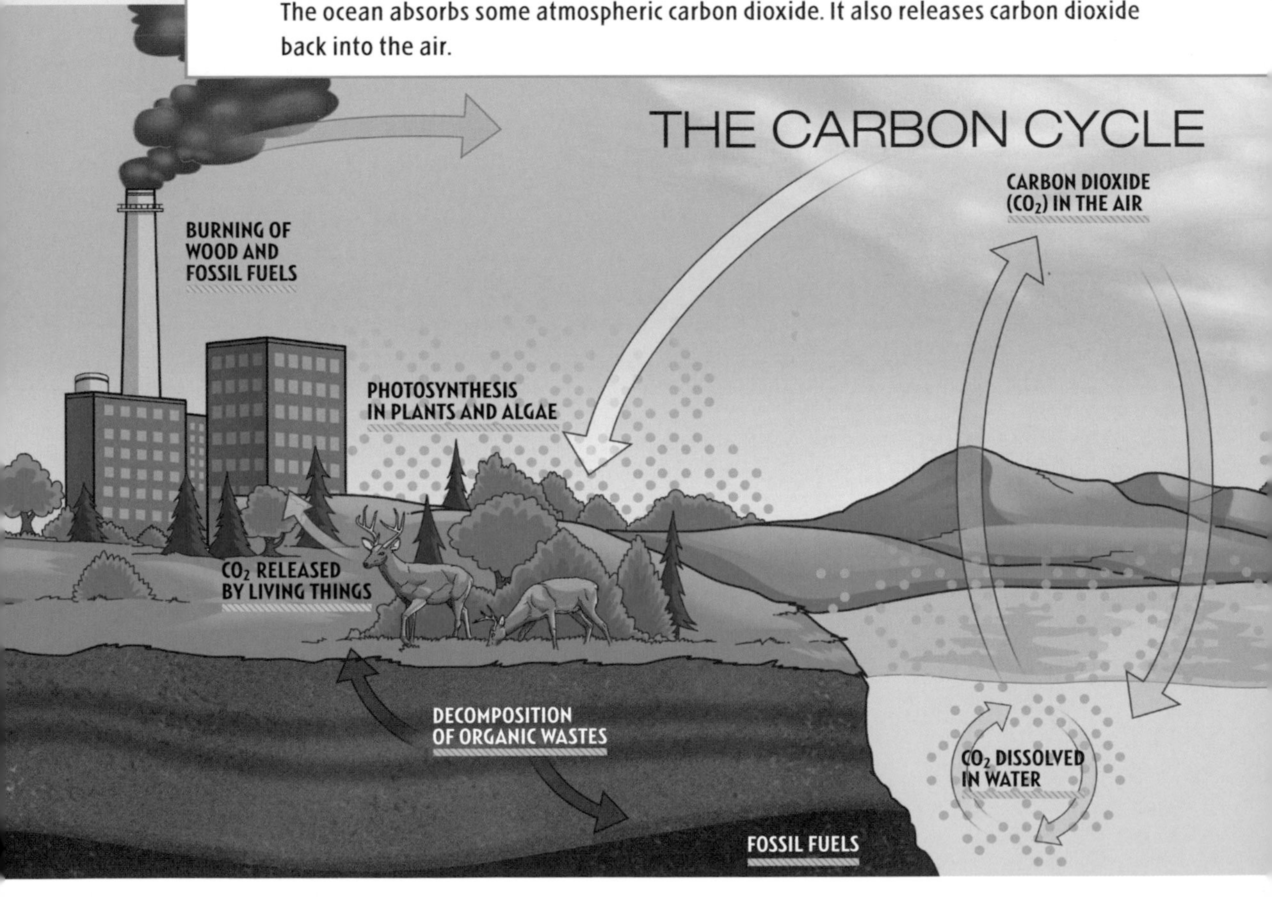

THE CARBON CYCLE

CARBON DIOXIDE
(CO_2) IN THE AIR

BURNING OF
WOOD AND
FOSSIL FUELS

PHOTOSYNTHESIS
IN PLANTS AND ALGAE

CO_2 RELEASED
BY LIVING THINGS

DECOMPOSITION
OF ORGANIC WASTES

CO_2 DISSOLVED
IN WATER

FOSSIL FUELS

the air you breathe out. They use the carbon dioxide to make sugar. Some of the sugar gets stored in the grass blades. A week later, you mow the grass. The clippings fall to the ground. Within a few days, they begin to decay. Some of the carbon in the decaying clippings moves back into the air as carbon dioxide. It's ready to be taken up by grass again.

Some of the rest of the carbon becomes part of the soil. That soil carbon may stay put for a while. A year or more could pass before it moves to another part of the carbon cycle. Other carbon can stay in the ground for much longer. Deep underground in some parts of the world are rich deposits of carbon. This carbon came from plants that died millions of years ago. They were covered with soil or water before they had a chance to decay. Instead, pressure and heat in the ground gradually turned them into fossil fuels such as oil, coal, and natural gas. Fossil fuels contain enormous amounts of carbon. All that carbon has been stored since dinosaurs roamed Earth.

WARMING POWER

Just how powerful is an atmospheric greenhouse effect? Some of our nearest neighbors in space have helped scientists answer that question. Mars *(above)*, the fourth planet from the sun, has a very thin atmosphere. It has almost no heat-trapping power. Almost all the heat coming from Mars' sun-warmed surface escapes into space. The result? The average surface temperature of Mars is a numbing −58°F (−50°C). Compare that to Venus, the second planet from the sun. Venus's atmosphere contains far more heat-trapping gas than Earth's atmosphere. The average temperature on Venus is a searing 778°F (414°C). That's hot enough to melt lead!

13

OTHER GREENHOUSE GASES

Two other naturally occurring substances are also important greenhouse gases. One is methane, another colorless, odorless gas. Methane is made of carbon and hydrogen. Most methane in the atmosphere comes from natural processes. Cows burp up methane as they digest their food. Decaying things release methane into the air. So does farming certain kinds of crops, especially rice.

Nitrous oxide is a greenhouse gas made of nitrogen and oxygen. This gas is colorless but has a slightly sweet smell. Bacteria in soils and in the ocean produce nitrous oxide. Livestock wastes, nitrogen fertilizers, and some industrial processes are also sources of nitrous oxide.

Several human-made chemicals also act as powerful greenhouse gases. Two of these chemicals are chlorofluorocarbons (CFCs) and hydrofluorocarbons (HFCs).

Cows graze in a field. As cows digest food, they burp up methane gas. Their waste also is a source of nitrous oxide.

TOO MUCH OF A GOOD THING

Water vapor, carbon dioxide, methane, and nitrous oxide all trap heat radiating from Earth's surface. These greenhouse gases are like a furnace's thermostat. If you turn up the thermostat, the room gets warmer. Adding more greenhouse gases to the atmosphere increases the atmosphere's heat-trapping power. They create a

GREENHOUSE GAS AND OZONE DESTROYER

In the last century, CFCs were used in refrigerators, air conditioners, and aerosol cans. Then scientists showed that these chemicals were escaping into the air. They were destroying ozone molecules. Ozone molecules form a protective layer in the stratosphere. This ozone layer absorbs powerful ultraviolet rays coming from the sun. It prevents most of these dangerous rays from reaching Earth's surface. A thinner ozone layer lets in more of the harmful rays. CFCs also turned out to be powerful, heat-trapping greenhouse gases. Many countries banned CFCs in the 1990s. But CFCs already in the atmosphere will stay there for many years.

stronger greenhouse effect.

A stronger greenhouse effect is what global warming is all about. Scientists are convinced that most of Earth's recent warming is the result of too much of a good thing. It's happening largely because huge amounts of greenhouse gases are entering the atmosphere. All those heat-trapping molecules are turning up Earth's thermostat. They are raising the planet's average surface temperature.

Of all the greenhouse gases, carbon dioxide is the biggest culprit in global warming. People do many things that release carbon dioxide into the air. But by far the most significant is burning fossil fuels. These fuels provide power around the planet. When they burn, however, most of the carbon they contain moves into the air in heat-trapping molecules of carbon dioxide.

15

CHAPTER TWO

TURNING UP THE HEAT

You flip a switch, and the lights come on. You turn on the television. You heat something in the microwave or play a game on your computer. Think of how many times you use electricity every day!

Where does the electricity come from? Most of it comes from power plants. And most power plants burn coal to generate electricity. The more electricity people use, the more fossil fuels must be burned to generate electricity. The result is that more carbon dioxide is released into the atmosphere.

16

POWERING A WAY OF LIFE

Cars, buses, and trucks run on gasoline or diesel fuel. Both come from oil, another fossil fuel. Many houses, schools, malls, hospitals, and offices have heating systems that burn oil or natural gas. Natural gas is a fossil fuel too.

Farmers planted and harvested the grains in your breakfast cereal with machines that burn diesel fuel. Factories powered by coal or oil made the package for the cereal. Trucks burning gasoline or diesel fuel transported the packages to the grocery store. And the store's bright lights, coolers, freezers, and cash registers all run on electricity.

The more electricity people use, the more fossil fuels must be burned to generate electricity.

Left: Smoke billows into the air at this coal-burning power station in Yunnan, China, in 2007. Coal-burning power stations release a lot of CO_2 into the atmosphere. *Below:* The cars, trucks, and buses on this six-lane highway in New Jersey all burn fossil fuels.

The world runs on fossil fuels. Worldwide, people burn hundreds of millions of tons of coal, oil, and natural gas every year. These carbon-rich fuels make our modern way of life possible. But this way of life has serious consequences for the planet.

THE FOSSIL FUEL REVOLUTION

Coal, oil, and other fossil fuels didn't always play such a big role in life. People didn't start using them in large amounts until the Industrial Revolution began. Up until that time, most things were made by hand. But around 1800, machines took over many kinds of manufacturing tasks. Factories full of machines sprang up in Europe and the United States. The energy to run all those machines and factories came from burning fossil fuels, especially coal.

The internal combustion engine arrived on the scene in the late 1800s. Powered by gasoline, this engine was used in the first successful automobiles. Within a few decades, millions of cars and trucks were on the road.

MAKING ELECTRICITY AROUND THE WORLD

As of 2007, 66 percent of the electricity generated worldwide came from burning coal, oil, and natural gas. In some parts of the world, fossil fuel use for generating electricity was far above this average. For example, 82 percent of the electricity produced in eastern and southern Asia came from fossil fuels. In the Middle East, it was a whopping 93 percent!

Over the past two hundred years, people have added enormous amounts of carbon dioxide to the atmosphere by burning fossil fuels. In 2005 the burning of fossil fuels put 7.9 billion tons (7.17 billion metric tons) of carbon, in the form of carbon dioxide, into the atmosphere. Carbon emissions increase every year.

TOP TEN CO$_2$ EMITTERS

Country	Total 2004 CO$_2$ emissions (in millions of metric tons)	Percent increase since 1990	2004 CO$_2$ emissions per person (in metric tons)
United States	6,046	25	20.6
China*	5,007	109	3.8
Russia	1,524	−23	10.6
India	1,342	97	1.2
Japan	1,257	17	9.9
Germany	808	−18	9.8
Canada	639	54	20.0
United Kingdom	587	1	9.8
South Korea	465	93	9.7
Italy	450	15	7.8

Source: United Nations Development Programme

* CO$_2$ emissions from China do not include emissions for Taiwan, Province of China.

The data in this chart refer to the CO$_2$ emissions from the use of fossil fuels, gas flaring, and production of cement. For many years, the United States was the world's largest emitter of carbon dioxide. In 2007 researchers announced that China had surpassed the United States. China emits more carbon dioxide than any other country. Most of China's carbon dioxide emissions come from burning coal and making cement.

OTHER SOURCES OF CARBON DIOXIDE

Burning fossil fuels isn't the only way people add lots of carbon dioxide to the atmosphere. To clear land for crops, farmers in many countries chop down trees and burn them. This deforestation adds a lot of carbon dioxide to the air. It also removes plants that would naturally take carbon dioxide out of the air for photosynthesis.

Tilling (digging up) the soil on farms releases carbon stored in soil. The carbon rises into the atmosphere as carbon dioxide. Certain industrial processes also add to the problem. For example, making cement releases large amounts of carbon dioxide.

Not all the carbon dioxide that's added to the atmosphere stays there. Some enters other parts of the carbon cycle. Plants absorb carbon dioxide from the air. So does the ocean. But human activities are adding far more carbon dioxide to the atmosphere than natural processes take out.

Fires burn in the Amazon rain forest as land is cleared for cattle grazing.

WHAT'S UP WITH OTHER GREENHOUSE GASES?

Carbon dioxide is not the only greenhouse gas on the rise. Methane and nitrous oxide are rapidly increasing in the atmosphere too. Methane traps twenty-three times as much heat in the atmosphere as carbon dioxide does. Nitrous oxide is three hundred times better at heat-trapping than carbon dioxide.

HOW MUCH IS UP THERE?

So how much carbon dioxide is in the atmosphere? And how fast is it increasing? A U.S. scientist, Dr. Charles David Keeling, started taking very accurate measurements of atmospheric carbon dioxide in the late 1950s. To get the best data, Keeling needed to sample the cleanest air possible. That meant taking measurements far away from cities, highways, and other sources of pollution.

In 1958 Keeling began measuring carbon dioxide from a laboratory on top of Mauna Loa, the highest mountain peak on the island of Hawaii. After just a few years, Keeling had conclusive proof. Atmospheric carbon dioxide was steadily increasing. Every year the amount of carbon dioxide in the atmosphere was higher than the year before.

That trend continues. When Keeling began his work, the level of atmospheric carbon dioxide was about 280 parts per million (ppm). (In every one million "parts" of air,

This graph shows the steady increase in atmospheric CO_2 since monitoring began in the late 1950s. Scientists often call this graph the Keeling Curve.

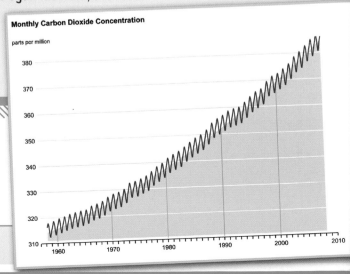

Monthly Carbon Dioxide Concentration

parts per million

380

370

360

350

340

330

320

310

1960   1970   1980   1990   2000   2010

280 were carbon dioxide molecules.) Since then that level has increased to over 380 ppm. That's more than at any point during the last 650,000 years.

CLUES FROM THE PAST

How do scientists know how much carbon dioxide was in the air long ago? They are able to measure carbon dioxide trapped in ancient ice.

Scientists drill into thick glaciers and ice sheets in different parts of the world. They take out long cylinders of ice. These ice cores contain many thin layers. Each layer represents one year's snowfall. The oldest layers of an ice core are at the bottom. The youngest are at the top.

The layers in an ice core contain tiny bubbles of trapped air. The bubbles are a record of what the air was like the year each layer formed. Scientists can measure the carbon dioxide in these air bubbles. That tells them how much carbon dioxide was in Earth's atmosphere at different times in the past.

22

FROZEN IN TIME

The longest, oldest ice cores come from very thick ice in Greenland and Antarctica. To date, the longest core ever drilled is from East Antarctica. The core contains layers of ice dating back at least 740,000 years.

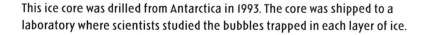
This ice core was drilled from Antarctica in 1993. The core was shipped to a laboratory where scientists studied the bubbles trapped in each layer of ice.

By measuring other gases in the bubbles, scientists can also tell what Earth's temperature was. Ice cores reveal that atmospheric carbon dioxide and Earth's average surface temperature are closely linked. The less carbon dioxide in the atmosphere, the lower the temperature. The more carbon dioxide, the higher the temperature. This connection between carbon dioxide and global temperature has held true for hundreds of thousands of years.

CARBON DIOXIDE AND GLOBAL WARMING

Since the Industrial Revolution began, levels of greenhouse gases have increased. So has Earth's temperature. Scientists know this is no coincidence. The link between greenhouse gases—especially carbon dioxide—and global warming is very strong.

In 2007 climate scientists worldwide agreed: Greenhouse gases that human activities are adding to the atmosphere are intensifying Earth's greenhouse effect. They are raising our planet's average surface temperature. And more warming is on the way. Just how much depends on what people around the world decide to do.

NOT JUST MOTHER NATURE

Until the early 2000s, global warming was a controversial topic. Initially many people, including some scientists, thought Earth's recent warming was just part of a natural cycle. For example, the amount of solar energy striking Earth increases and decreases over a period of about eleven years. This variation is due to sunspots. Sunspots are cooler patches that form on the sun's surface. When there are more sunspots, less solar energy reaches Earth and vice versa. Natural cycles such as this do affect global temperature. But nearly all scientists agree that natural cycles alone cannot explain global warming. The evidence is overwhelming that human activities are responsible for most of the current warming.

CHAPTER THREE

EARTH'S CHANGING CLIMATE

So what? What if the world is getting warmer by a few degrees? How much difference could a few degrees make?

In fact, they can make a world of difference. About eighteen thousand years ago, Earth's average temperature was only slightly cooler than it was in the past century. Yet vast glaciers covered large parts of the Northern Hemisphere. In North America, these great ice sheets extended from northern Canada to where Kansas and Oklahoma are.

The glaciers formed because a few degrees of cooling changed Earth's climate. Climate is the average weather a place has over a long period of time. During the time of the glaciers, winters were much colder. Summers were cooler and shorter. More snow fell than melted. Glaciers grew very thick and covered immense areas of land.

Then, very gradually, Earth's average surface temperature increased a few degrees. The ice sheets slowly melted and retreated. By about ten thousand years ago, the only large areas of ice left were on mountain tops and near the poles.

The melting ice in Greenland is shown in both of these images. *Left:* A stream of meltwater cascades off part of the Greenland ice sheet. *Below:* Water pours off an iceberg that broke off a glacier in Greenland.

EXTENT OF GLACIERS IN THE LAST ICE AGE

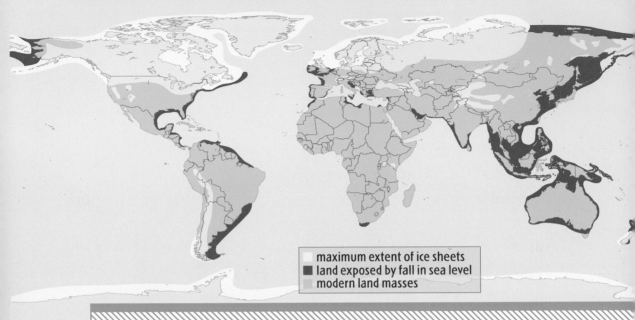

■ maximum extent of ice sheets
■ land exposed by fall in sea level
■ modern land masses

About eighteen thousand years ago, a cooling of Earth's average surface temperature led to global climate change. Huge sheets of glacial ice covered large parts of several continents. So much water froze into ice that the sea level fell along many coastlines.

Recent global warming is raising Earth's temperature very quickly. Many scientists believe climate will change worldwide in response to this sudden warming. They've found a lot of evidence that it is already changing.

CLIMATE MODELS

When Earth's temperature began rising, scientists wanted to know how that warming might change the climate. They also wondered how climate changes could affect life on Earth.

Climate isn't something you can study under a microscope or in a laboratory. Scientists created models of Earth's climate system. Climate models are very complex computer programs. Scientists build climate models by dividing Earth's surface and atmosphere into blocks, or cells, within the program. Then they develop sets of math equations that describe the conditions in each cell. These equations reflect how temperature, humidity, wind speed, ocean currents, and other factors interact. More equations link all the cells. In that way, they work together as a whole, like Earth's real climate system.

Weather models are a bit like climate models. Meteorologists are scientists who study and predict the weather. They enter current weather data into weather models. Then the models make a projection based on the data. They show, or forecast, what the next few days of weather will be like.

CLIMATE VS. WEATHER

Don't confuse climate and weather. Weather is the warm, cold, sunny, or rainy condition of the atmosphere at any given time. Weather changes quickly from day to day. Climate is the typical weather a place experiences from year to year over a long time.

27

This meteorologist is studying weather projections made by a computer weather model. Climate scientists use climate models to project how global warming will likely affect Earth.

Similarly, scientists use climate models to make climate projections. These are predictions about what the climate may be like in the next decade or century. However, predicting climate is much more complicated than figuring out tomorrow's weather. So climate models are much more complex than weather models.

Making accurate projections of how global warming may change the climate worldwide is enormously difficult. Early climate models were rough. They included the best data scientists could gather at the time. But for some parts of the climate system, data simply weren't available.

By the end of the twentieth century, however, climate models had improved a lot. New satellites and other advanced tools collected much more data. They also collected new kinds of data. Modern climate models are much better at simulating Earth's climate system than earlier versions. Computers that run climate models are faster and more powerful too.

To make climate projections, scientists program a model to test what climate would be like under different conditions. For example, a model could test the effects of carbon emissions decreasing, increasing, or staying the same over the next ten years. How much would Earth warm in each case by the year 2100? How would the resulting warmth change the climate worldwide?

Climate isn't something you can study under a microscope or in a laboratory.

Climate models still aren't perfect. They never will be. But scientists are confident in the projections modern climate models are making. Many predictions have already been confirmed by observations. In other words, what the models are saying will happen has already begun to happen. The following projections and evidence will give you an idea of what has happened already and what may be still to come.

GLOBAL SURFACE TEMPERATURE

Projections

If people worldwide cut carbon emissions drastically and soon, levels of atmospheric carbon dioxide might stay below 400 ppm. That would limit further global warming to about 3.2°F (1.8°C) by 2100. But if people keep burning fossil fuels at the current rate, carbon dioxide levels could reach 780 ppm by 2100. That could raise Earth's temperature by as much as 11.5°F (6.4°C). Our planet would be warmer than it has been in more than one million years.

Models show that different parts of the planet may warm more or less than the global average. All climate models project that places near the North Pole and South Pole will warm the most.

Evidence

Earth's average surface temperature increased 1.4°F (0.8°C) during the twentieth century. The Arctic warmed nearly 5°F (2.8°C) during the same period. The Antarctic Peninsula has warmed almost as much as the Arctic. This finger of land juts out from Antarctica toward South America. All told, Earth is already warmer than it has been during the last ten thousand years.

Melting sea ice breaks up in the Arctic Ocean north of Canada.

OCEAN TEMPERATURE

Projections

Climate models forecast that as the air near Earth's surface warms, so will the ocean. Models also predict that the ocean will warm fastest near the equator. However, water warms more slowly than land or air. The larger the body of water, the slower the change. And the ocean is really big. It covers three-quarters of Earth's surface and is 13,000 feet (4 km) deep on average. So any change in its temperature should be very gradual.

30

Evidence

Scientists have determined that since the 1960s, the ocean has warmed 0.18°F (0.10°C) from the surface down to about 2,297 feet (700 meters). That may not seem like much. But an enormous amount of heat is needed to raise the ocean's temperature even just a little. And as predicted, tropical ocean waters have warmed more than those nearer the poles.

TAKING THE OCEAN'S TEMPERATURE

In 2000 scientists from several different countries began a project to measure ocean temperature as precisely as possible. The project, called Argo, uses more than three thousand instrument-packed floats. Argo floats *(shown above)* are bobbing on ocean waves worldwide. They measure water temperature and saltiness down to a depth of 6,562 feet (2,000 m).

MELTING ICE

Projections

Models project that as global temperatures rise, sea ice, ice sheets, and glaciers will begin to melt. Melting should be most severe in polar regions. That's because warming there will be the greatest.

Melting mountain glaciers will directly affect water supplies in some areas. For example, the Himalaya Mountains have more than fifteen thousand glaciers. Millions of people in several countries, including China, depend on the glaciers' melted runoff for drinking water. Climate models predict that 80 percent of Himalayan glaciers will be gone by 2100. As the glaciers disappear, so will the drinking water.

Evidence

Since about 1978, satellites have been tracking sea ice in the Arctic Ocean. Satellite pictures show that the area covered by ice year-round is steadily shrinking. Melting has increased dramatically since about 2000. Between 2005 and 2007, the year-round ice has shrunk by an area the size of Texas and California combined. And in the summer of 2007, the area covered by Arctic sea ice was the smallest it's ever been. Some scientists think that the ice may completely disappear by the summer of 2013. The ice cap will exist only in winter.

Ice is also melting on the opposite end of the world. Scientists have studied more than 250 glaciers on

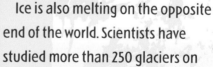

These satellite images show recent changes in Arctic sea ice. The image on top shows the sea ice area in summer 1979. The image on the bottom shows the sea ice area in summer 2007.

the Antarctic Peninsula. They've found that since the mid-1900s, 87 percent of the glaciers have melted significantly. On both sides of the peninsula, ice shelves extend out into the ocean. Warmer temperatures are weakening the ice shelves. Several state-sized pieces of these ice shelves have broken off since the 1990s. The massively thick ice sheets that cover Antarctica's interior are also showing signs of melting around their edges.

After Antarctica, Greenland has the world's second-largest ice sheet. But global warming has triggered unexpectedly rapid melting of Greenland's ice. Scientists calculate that since 2006, the island has lost roughly 165 billion tons (150 billion metric tons) of ice per year. That is twice as much ice as is in all the glaciers in the Alps, Europe's largest mountain range.

Glaciers in the Alps are also melting. That's true of most mountain glaciers worldwide. Teams of scientists have reported dramatic shrinking of glaciers in Alaska. Montana's Glacier National Park may have no glaciers left by 2030. Mountain glaciers are also disappearing in Peru, Chile, Nepal, Tanzania, Switzerland, and other countries.

NORTHWEST PASSAGE OPENS!

In the summer of 2007, so much Arctic sea ice melted that open water linked the Atlantic and Pacific Oceans. For centuries, sailors searched for a "northwest passage" that would have made such a boat trip possible. But sea ice always blocked the way. Climate models projected the passage would eventually open as global temperatures rose. But none predicted it would happen so soon.

SEA LEVEL RISE

Projections

Sea level is a measure of how much water is in the ocean. Sea level measurements show how high onto land the ocean reaches. All climate models project that global warming will raise sea level worldwide. This sea level rise has two causes. First, as water warms, its molecules spread out. So water already in the ocean takes up more space. Second, when ice sheets and glaciers melt, water that had been stored on land is added to the ocean. This increases the ocean's total volume. The more water that's added, the higher sea level will rise.

Rising sea level will threaten people living on islands and near the ocean. Worldwide, eleven of the world's fifteen largest cities are on a coast. Dramatic sea level rise won't happen anywhere overnight. But it could ultimately force millions, even billions, of people to move to higher ground. Rising seas would also flood thousands of square miles of coastal cropland. And the salt water would contaminate freshwater sources. So fewer food and drinking water supplies will be available.

Evidence

Sea level rose more than 6 inches (15 centimeters) between the late 1800s and 2000. The rate of increase sped up toward the end of the twentieth century. Between 1993 and 2005, sea level rose about 0.1 inches (3 millimeters) per year. If that trend continues, sea level is likely to be 11.2 to 17.2 inches (28 to 43 cm) higher by 2100. But this projection is very uncertain. It all depends on how much land ice melts and flows into the sea. If the entire Greenland ice sheet melts, that water alone would raise sea level by 24 feet (7.3 m). Melting of the Antarctic ice sheets would raise sea level by several hundred feet more.

A scientist measures the ground-level temperature on the tundra in northern Alaska.

THAWING TUNDRA

Projections

The Arctic tundra lies south of the Arctic Ocean. It is an immense, treeless landscape. Typically during summer, only the top few inches of tundra soil thaw. Below that the ground remains frozen. This permanently frozen soil is permafrost. Climate models project that as Arctic regions warm, much of the tundra's permafrost will melt.

Evidence

The climate on the tundra is changing rapidly. Permafrost is melting in northern Alaska and northern Canada. In western Siberia, scientists have discovered that roughly 386,000 square miles (about 1 million sq. km) of permafrost have thawed. If warming continues as expected, 90 percent of the permafrost in all Arctic regions could melt by 2100.

Tundra thawing is more than a problem of soggy ground. Tundra soil is rich in dead plant and animal matter. That means it's rich in carbon. Scientists estimate that worldwide, permafrost holds 992 billion tons (900 billion metric tons) of carbon. As long as the soil is frozen, the dead matter doesn't decay. But as tundra soil melts, decay processes get under way. Melting permafrost is releasing huge amounts of both carbon dioxide and methane from decay into the atmosphere.

MORE SEVERE WEATHER

Projections

Climate models project that global warming will change weather patterns worldwide. As temperatures rise, moderate weather patterns will tip toward extreme weather patterns. Severe storms and heat waves are likely to be more common. Changes in precipitation will increase chances of flooding in some places. They'll bring droughts to others.

Heat waves, droughts, and floods can have serious consequences for people. Because of climate change, at least 75 million people in Africa could face severe water shortages due to drought by 2020. Where African farmers depend on rainfall for their crops, food supplies may drop by 50 percent.

Heat waves and droughts spark wildfires. These fires could destroy large parts of many North American forests in the coming years. More fires will likely threaten cities, especially in drought-prone areas like Southern California. As glaciers disappear in the Rocky Mountains, people in western states may face severe water shortages and more frequent and severe wildfires. In the U.S. Southwest, drought conditions may become permanent. People living in cities there could find it difficult to get enough water. Farmers and ranchers might eventually be unable to raise crops and livestock.

These farmers stand in a parched field in Australia in 2006.

In the future, increased flooding in parts of the world will likely drive millions of people from their homes, at least temporarily. Crops will be destroyed and topsoil washed away. Floods also spread life-threatening diseases.

Evidence

Hurricanes form over warm oceans. The storms draw strength from the heat in surface waters. As the ocean warms, it may spawn more powerful hurricanes. Scientists don't link any individual weather event, including a hurricane, directly to global warming. But several science teams report an increase in the number of powerful hurricanes since the 1990s. Other scientists, however, say the evidence isn't strong enough. More information is needed to determine if global warming is the cause of this increase.

Heat waves do appear to be on the rise. In August 2003, Western Europe experienced its worst heat wave on record. More than thirty-five thousand people died as a result of record-breaking temperatures. In 2006 heat waves struck Europe again, along with the United States. In 2007 unusually severe heat

Young people in Lahore, Pakistan, cool off in a canal during a June 2007 heat wave.

waves blasted India, Pakistan, and parts of Russia. Southeastern Europe and parts of North Africa also roasted in scorching temperatures.

Heavy rains and floods seem to be becoming more common. In 2005 Mumbai, India, received a world-record 37 inches (94 cm) of rain in twenty-four hours. In 2006 in Hawaii, nearly 11 feet (3.4 m) of rain fell on Mount Waialeale in just six weeks. In 2007 record-breaking floods ravaged parts of the United Kingdom, the United States, Indonesia, India, Bangladesh, and Nepal.

Meanwhile, droughts have been increasingly widespread in Europe, Asia, Canada, and parts of Africa since the 1990s. Since 2001 Australia has suffered from the worst drought in its history.

CHANGING SEASONS

Projections

As temperatures warm, seasons will change in many parts of the world. Models predict that winters will be warmer and shorter in many places. Spring will come earlier. Summers should be hotter and last longer.

For people living in Arctic regions, a warmer climate and longer summers will bring great change. As snow and ice melt, people will lose their traditional way of life. In temperate (mild-weather) regions, a longer summer growing season could mean higher crop yields for farmers. Some crops also may grow faster because of more carbon dioxide in the air. But weeds will grow faster too.

THE NENANA ICE CLASSIC

Since 1917 people in the village of Nenana, Alaska, have been betting on the exact minute when spring will arrive each year. The agreed-upon start of spring is the moment the ice breaks up on the nearby Tanana River. For scientists the Nenana Ice Classic, as this contest is called, is a source of data about climate change. Based on event records, spring arrives ten days earlier around Nenana than it did in 1960.

An Inupiat hunter walks on melting sea ice on the Chukchi Sea in Alaska. The Inupiat used to use dogsleds or snow machines for their hunting on the ice. Melting sea ice has forced them to drag boats across patches of ice to open water.

Evidence

Spring snowmelt in the western United States starts roughly a month earlier than it did in the early 1970s. In many northern parts of the country, lakes and rivers thaw several days to a week earlier in spring. In Europe, spring begins one to two weeks earlier than in the 1970s.

ANIMALS AND PLANTS

Projections

Changes in weather patterns and seasons will impact many plants and animals. Models predict that plant populations will tend to move toward the poles. Migrating animals may change the timing of their travels. Or they may change the routes they take to and from their summer and winter homes. Entire populations of animals may also move permanently to escape too-high temperatures. However, not all species will be able to move or move fast enough. These species may not survive. Researchers estimate global warming may drive 15 to 37 percent of North American plant and animal species to extinction by 2050. Some harmful species, such as malaria-carrying mosquitoes, may invade areas where they never lived before.

Evidence

Scientists in the United States recently studied 1,400 kinds of plants and animals. They found that more than 80 percent start their spring activities earlier than they used to. On average, trees bud out, frogs mate, insects hatch, and birds nest more than a week earlier than they did in the 1960s. A 2003 study showed that 1,700 plant and animal species had moved toward the poles. They shifted about 4 miles (6.4 km) per decade closer to the poles over the last fifty years.

In addition, at least twenty-one kinds of ocean fish have left waters that have become too warm. Some moved closer to the poles. Others headed for deeper, cooler water.

NO GOING BACK

Global warming and climate change have the potential to drastically change life on Earth. In the coming years, some of the effects of global warming might not be as bad as models project. But others might turn out to be much worse.

We can't reverse the situation. Earth is already warming. Some degree of climate change is inevitable. But the future isn't set in stone. By acting quickly to reduce greenhouse gases, the world still has time to avoid the worst that global warming might bring.

NATURAL CLIMATE-CHANGING FORCES

Many natural forces shape climate. When volcanoes erupt, they send dust high into the atmosphere. That volcanic dust can block solar energy and slightly cool Earth's surface. Patterns of winds and ocean currents also influence climate worldwide. When these patterns change, so does climate. One such change is the El Niño-Southern Oscillation (ENSO). ENSO is a set of changes in the Pacific Ocean's wind and water. These changes take place every few years. They affect the weather on several continents that border the Pacific. Other forces of natural climate shift are changes in Earth's tilt on its axis or in its path of orbit around the sun. But as with recent global warming, natural forces alone can't explain recent climate change. Human activities are largely to blame.

CHAPTER FOUR

TACKLING A GLOBAL PROBLEM

Global warming may seem like a new problem. But scientists began raising concerns about it in the 1950s. However, people and governments worldwide mostly ignored them.

ONE HOT SUMMER

In the 1980s, Dr. James Hansen, a U.S. climate expert, started speaking out publicly about global warming. He maintained that warming was not just a remote possibility. It was very likely to happen as a result of fossil fuel use worldwide. Hansen testified before Congress in the summer of 1988. He warned that as the world warmed, climate would almost certainly change.

That same summer, the United States suffered a record-breaking heat wave. Both the heat and the issue of global warming made headlines. A number of climate experts called for governments to take action to reduce greenhouse gases. But a few scientists downplayed the problem. So did many government officials and industry leaders. They cautioned that cutting back on using fossil fuels would harm the economy. Industries would shut down. People would lose their jobs. Politicians claimed there was too little evidence to support global warming hypotheses. It was better, they said, not to act.

Left: Dr. James Hansen, shown here in 2006, talks about changing weather patterns. Hansen started speaking out about global warming and climate change in the 1980s. *Below:* A power station rises in the distance behind an open-pit coal mine in Germany.

Concerned scientists didn't give up. They worked with the World Meteorological Organization and the United Nations Environment Programme to establish the Intergovernmental Panel on Climate Change (IPCC). The IPCC objectively reviews research about global warming and climate change. It studies the potential impacts of climate change and ways to reduce those impacts.

THE IPCC

The IPCC brings together hundreds of climate scientists from many countries. The scientists form three main working groups. Each group reviews scientific knowledge of a different aspect of global warming and climate change. The IPCC has published major reports on climate change in 1990, 1995, 2001, and 2007.

42

THE KYOTO PROTOCOL AND BEYOND

Following the formation of the IPCC, several international conferences about global warming took place. In 1992 the Earth Summit, held in Brazil, produced the first international treaty on climate change. This agreement, called the United Nations Framework Convention on Climate Change (UNFCCC), outlined voluntary guidelines for reducing carbon emissions. Nearly

UNITED NATIONS CONFERENCE ON ENVIRONMENT AND DEVELOPMENT
Rio de Janeiro 3–14 June 1992

The Earth Summit in Brazil in 1992 brought world leaders together to talk about climate change.

Members of the United Nations and the IPCC show their latest report on climate change at a conference on global warming in 2007.

two hundred countries signed the treaty. However, few actually followed the guidelines. Cutting emissions required making changes, especially in industries. The changes cost money. Many governments felt they couldn't justify the cost.

The UNFCCC was a starting point. But stronger measures were needed. In 1997 a number of countries approved an addition to the treaty, called the Kyoto Protocol. The Kyoto Protocol legally requires countries to limit greenhouse gas emissions. The Kyoto Protocol gives specific goals for lowering emissions between 2008 and 2012. Most of the world's nations eventually agreed to the Kyoto Protocol. But a few countries, including the United States and Australia, did not. Nevertheless, the Kyoto Protocol went into effect in early 2005. All the participating countries are working to meet their emission goals.

In 2007 representatives from over 180 countries met in Bali, Indonesia, for another climate conference. The conference ended with an agreement by all the participants, including the United States. They agreed to work together on a global plan to address climate change issues by 2009.

European countries have taken major steps in cutting greenhouse gas emissions. The twenty-seven member states that form the European Union set up the Emission Trading Scheme (ETS). It is the first international trading system for carbon dioxide emissions. The ETS sets limits on large carbon dioxide emitters such as coal-burning power plants. If a plant goes over its limit, it must buy carbon credits from other companies (or countries) that pollute less to cover the excess. Typically, plants don't want to spend money buying more carbon credits. So the system encourages them to keep emission levels low. In 2007 more than ten thousand European power plants and other industrial CO$_2$ emitters were part of the ETS.

CARBON TRADING

Exchanging carbon credits is called carbon trading. It has become a big business. Here's how it works: A company (or country) that goes over its carbon dioxide emission limit can buy or trade for carbon credits from a seller. The seller might be a developing country that emits little carbon dioxide. Or it could be a company that emits less than its limit. Carbon trading is supposed to help reduce carbon dioxide emissions. It's also supposed to encourage use of cleaner energy, such as solar and wind power. Supporters of carbon trading say it is helping to lower emissions. However, critics say the system has too many loopholes and limits need to be stricter.

STATES TAKE THE LEAD

The U.S. government has been slow to tackle global warming and climate change issues. But many states are taking matters into their own hands. Several are leading the way in trying to reduce carbon emissions in the country.

In 2003 the Regional Greenhouse Gas Initiative began. It is a carbon credit trading program for power plants in northeastern states. Power plants receive carbon credits that allow them to release a certain amount of carbon dioxide. (Each credit allows for the release of 1 ton (0.91 metric ton) of carbon dioxide.) If a plant releases more carbon dioxide than it has credits for, it must buy additional credits from plants that release less than their limit. Those that break the rules face heavy penalties.

In 2002 California passed a state law to cut greenhouse emissions from cars. The Clean Cars law was the first of its kind in the nation. It imposed stricter fuel economy and emissions standards on new cars.

SOLUTIONS IN CALIFORNIA

California is the world's twelfth-largest greenhouse gas emitter. In 2005 California's Governor Arnold Schwarzenegger proposed bold targets to reduce the state's greenhouse gas emissions. A year later, the California legislature approved the California Global Warming Solutions Act. The act set emissions limits that ensure the state's greenhouse gas emissions are reduced to 1990 levels by the year 2020. Schwarzenegger signed the bill into law in September 2006. Other states are considering similar legislation.

California governor Arnold Schwarzenegger signs the Global Warming Solutions Act in 2006.

But in 2004, automakers sued California over the law. They said that only the federal government can regulate fuel economy and therefore emissions. California fought back. It took the case all the way to the U.S. Supreme Court. In 2007 the Court ruled that carbon dioxide is a pollutant. That meant that California and other states have the right to regulate it. Eighteen other states quickly adopted the Clean Cars law too.

In December 2007, however, the U.S. Environmental Protection Agency blocked California's Clean Cars law. It was an unexpected move, since part of the EPA's job is to help limit pollutants. California, along with a dozen other states and several environmental groups, quickly responded. In 2008 they filed a lawsuit to require the EPA to comply with the Supreme Court's earlier ruling. Stay tuned!

MAYORS MAKING A DIFFERENCE

On February 16, 2005, Seattle mayor Greg Nickels launched the U.S. Mayors Climate Protection Agreement. That was the same day that the Kyoto Protocol went into effect. The idea behind the agreement was to get leaders from all fifty states to reduce greenhouse gas emissions to 1990 levels by 2012. As of 2008, more than eight hundred mayors of cities across the United States had signed on.

Under the agreement, participants promise to work to reduce carbon emissions in their communities to the target levels set by the Kyoto Protocol. They agree to urge the state and federal governments to do the same. And they agree to encourage members of Congress to pass greenhouse gas laws that will create a national carbon trading system.

Governments are slowly addressing the global warming problem. Placing limits on greenhouse gas emissions is a first step. But governments, industries, and individuals can all do more.

Governments are slowly addressing the global warming problem.

Smoke billows out of chimneys at a power plant in Mongolia in 2007. Countries around the world are working on the problem of global warming. Efforts include reducing emissions from power plants.

CHAPTER FIVE

STRATEGIES FOR A SUSTAINABLE FUTURE

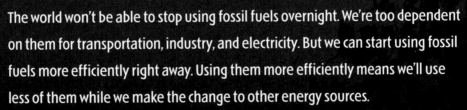

Greenhouse gases must be cut as quickly as possible to slow global warming. How can the world do this? For starters, we can use fewer fossil fuels. And we can switch to other sources of energy that don't release carbon dioxide into the air.

IMPROVING ENERGY EFFICIENCY

The world won't be able to stop using fossil fuels overnight. We're too dependent on them for transportation, industry, and electricity. But we can start using fossil fuels more efficiently right away. Using them more efficiently means we'll use less of them while we make the change to other energy sources.

For starters, we can use fewer fossil fuels.

Replacing gas-guzzling cars and trucks with fuel-efficient vehicles is one way to start. Smaller gas-powered cars are growing in popularity. Smaller vehicles are more fuel efficient than larger trucks and SUVs. Hybrid cars use less fuel than strictly gas-powered cars of any size. That means fewer greenhouse gases entering the air. Most hybrid cars are powered by gasoline and electricity from a rechargeable battery. The battery charges as the car

Left: This hybrid vehicle from Mazda can run on either gasoline or hydrogen gas. When hydrogen combines with oxygen from the air, energy is released to power the car. *Below:* The Toyota Prius cars are popular hybrid vehicles on the market. They run on gasoline and battery power.

LIGHTS OUT!

In 2007 Australia passed a law to ban the sale of incandescent lightbulbs nationwide. Australians are replacing their old bulbs with energy-efficient compact fluorescent bulbs (CFLs). CFLs use about 70 percent less electricity than incandescent bulbs. A similar change in the United States would have huge effects. If every U.S. household replaced three of its incandescent bulbs with CFLs, carbon dioxide emissions would drop by 23 million tons (20.9 million metric tons) per year. That's like saving all the emissions from eleven coal-fired power plants!

moves. About two dozen brands of hybrid cars are already on the market.

Appliances we use every day run on electricity. Refrigerators and air conditioners, ovens and clothes dryers, and water heaters and washing machines all need electric power. So do lightbulbs. (How many lightbulbs are in your house?) Switching to energy-efficient appliances and bulbs can save a lot of electricity. And that reduces the amount of fossil fuels we use.

ALTERNATIVE FUELS

Alternative fuels can be used as substitutes for fossil fuels. Two alternative fuels, ethanol and biodiesel, are already sold at gas stations. Burning alternative fuels still releases carbon dioxide into the air. But not as much as burning fossil fuels does.

Ethanol is an alcohol-based fuel. It's made from starchy crops like corn, barley, and wheat. It can also be produced from cornstalks and other plant wastes. Most of the ethanol made in the United States comes from corn. Pure ethanol isn't a substitute for gasoline. But ethanol-gasoline blends are common. You probably see one called E10 at gas stations. E10 is 10 percent ethanol and 90 percent gasoline.

E85 is available at this gas station in Wisconsin, right next to diesel and unleaded gasoline fuels.

Another less common blend is E85. It's 85 percent ethanol and 15 percent gasoline. Ordinary car engines can't run on E85. But flex-fuel vehicles (FFVs) can. FFVs run on gasoline, ethanol, or any blend of the two. It doesn't cost much to turn a regular car into a flex-fuel car. Several million FFVs are already on U.S. roads.

Biodiesel is an alternative fuel for cars and trucks that use diesel fuel. It's made from a mixture of vegetable oil and alcohol. In the United States, most biodiesel is made from soybean oil.

ENERGY CONSERVATION

Conserving energy means using less of it. The less energy we use, the fewer greenhouse gases will enter the atmosphere. We can conserve energy by driving more efficient cars and driving less in general. We can avoid leaving lights on when no one's home or turn down the thermostat before going to bed. We can also make conscious choices about other things we do and how we do them.

For example, people have a choice about how to get to school or work. Driving a car is a choice. But it means a lot of greenhouse gases get added to the air. Taking public transportation is a better choice for Earth's atmosphere. True, a bus or train also burns fuel and releases carbon dioxide. But emissions from one bus are better than those of several dozen cars. The most Earth-friendly choice is to walk or ride a bike. It's slower and probably more work, especially if there are hills along the way! But it's a completely emissions-free way to get around.

This city bus uses hybrid technology to run. In addition to reducing pollution, hybrid buses can save city governments money on the cost of fuel.

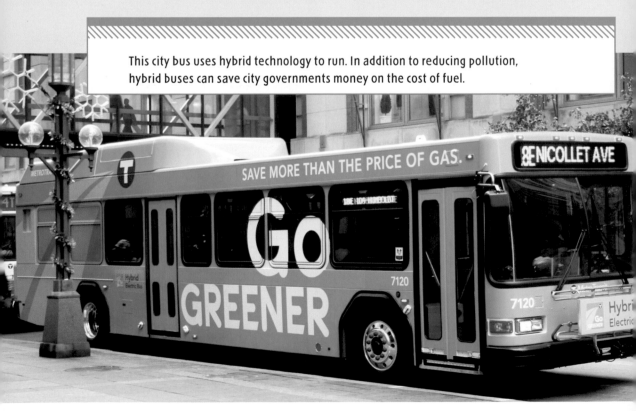

MAKING A DIFFERENCE

Global warming may seem like a huge problem that only large organizations or governments can solve. But individuals really can make a difference. When Sarah Ferriter was a student at the University of Southern Maine (USM), she wanted to help reduce greenhouse gas emissions. The university's shuttle buses burned diesel fuel. Sarah thought the buses should change to biodiesel. But biodiesel is more expensive than diesel fuel. So Sarah proposed that every student at USM pay a 1 dollar fee per year to offset the cost. Students loved the idea. So did the administration, which simply covered the extra cost with school funds. USM's buses switched to biodiesel. The university uses biodiesel to heat campus buildings too. Just one person brought about this big change.

Reusing and recycling are also easy ways to conserve energy. Almost everything we use, from paper to plastics, requires energy to make. Using something again and again means a new one doesn't have to be manufactured. Recycling materials like plastics, aluminum, and paper conserves oil, natural resources, and forests. Plus, it saves all the energy needed to transform raw materials into finished products. The savings can

53

A pile of newspapers is ready to be recycled.

be huge. For instance, for every 1 pound (0.5 kilograms) of paper that is used on both sides and then recycled—instead of used once and thrown away—2.5 pounds (1.1 kg) of greenhouse gases are saved.

RENEWABLE ENERGY

Conserving energy reduces the use of fossil fuels, which are a limited resource. It buys time in our warming world to develop renewable energy sources. These include solar, wind, geothermal, hydropower, and biomass. Except for biomass, these energy sources don't add carbon dioxide or other greenhouse gases to the air. And because they're renewable, we'll never run out of them!

54

THE POWER TOWER

Spain's PS10 solar power tower began operating in 2007. A total of 624 huge, movable mirrors (called heliostats) concentrate the sun's rays on top of a thirty-five-story tower. There, a turbine drives a generator to produce electricity. When running at full capacity, the power tower will produce enough electricity to run six hundred thousand homes. And all without releasing a single puff of greenhouse gas!

This solar power tower near Seville, Spain, opened in March 2007.

Solar power is energy from the sun. It can be harnessed in several ways. The first is by using solar panels (called photovoltaic cells). These convert the energy in sunlight directly into electricity. Solar panels used to be very expensive. But new kinds are much cheaper and more efficient. They're also thinner, smaller, and more flexible. Solar hot water systems use the sun's energy to heat water. Solar-thermal power stations typically use mirrors to concentrate solar energy, which powers a turbine. The turbine then spins to generate electricity.

Wind power is renewable energy from moving air. Tall wind turbines stand in open spaces, where the wind spins the turbine blades to generate electricity. Giant wind turbines are becoming part of the landscape in many places. Groups of wind turbines are sometimes called wind farms.

Geothermal energy is natural heat from inside Earth. In some places, intense geothermal heat is stored in steam or hot water deep underground. Geothermal energy can run power plants that give off little or no carbon dioxide. In some places, people use geothermal energy to heat buildings directly.

These wind turbines on a wind farm in California supply energy to the Oakland area.

Moving water also has power. (You know this if you've ever paddled a canoe upstream.) Hydropower is energy captured from water flowing along a river or surging out of a dam. The back-and-forth movement of ocean waves is a source of water power too. Waves can drive turbines to produce electricity. So can tides. Tides are the regular rising and falling of the ocean along a shoreline. In some places, changing tides create strong currents. Put a tidal turbine in the water, and the turbine's spinning blades will change the water's energy into electricity.

Electricity from grass clippings and wood chips may sound strange. But those wastes, called biomass, were once parts of plants. The plants captured energy from sunlight and stored it in leaves, stems, and trunks. When biomass burns in huge boilers, the heat that's released can turn water into steam. The steam can turn turbines to generate electricity. Burning biomass does release carbon dioxide. But the amount released is the same as was removed from the air during the plant's lifetime. So biomass is considered a "carbon-neutral" source of power.

56

CARBON-NEUTRAL LIFESTYLES

People can be carbon neutral too. They can try to adopt a carbon-neutral lifestyle. That means taking creative steps to get rid of, or cancel out, everyday activities that generate carbon dioxide.

Dried hay and plant stalks are covered by a tarp and tires outside a bioenergy plant in Germany.

The first step toward a carbon-neutral lifestyle is to calculate your carbon footprint. That's a measure of how much carbon dioxide you put into the air every day. It's usually expressed as tons of carbon dioxide or tons of carbon emitted per year. Businesses, cities, and countries can have carbon footprints too.

Next, you try to offset your carbon footprint. This means doing things that take carbon dioxide out of the air to make up for things that add carbon dioxide to it. Conserving energy can help offset carbon emissions. So can buying carbon credits. Individuals can do this, not just companies and countries. All sorts of projects allow people to purchase carbon credits. Buying carbon credits "retires" credits that would otherwise be traded to countries or companies. Retiring credits makes them harder to get. There are fewer to go around. So it encourages countries and companies to reduce their emissions. That reduction of emissions offsets the carbon footprint of the person who bought the carbon credit.

You can also reduce your carbon footprint by getting involved in environmental projects that help reduce emissions. For example, you can buy carbon credits from an organization that plants trees. The money goes to plant trees that will take up carbon dioxide from the air. The more credits you buy, the more trees get planted and the more carbon is offset.

TOWARD A GLOBAL SOLUTION

Global warming is a global problem. Addressing it requires a global solution. People everywhere must stop adding greenhouse gases to the air. We must find ways to replace fossil fuels with clean, renewable energy sources.

The world has the technology and the creativity to find these solutions. But we have to be willing to make the effort. And we have to take action soon. If we don't, the amount of atmospheric carbon dioxide will keep increasing. Earth's greenhouse effect will keep intensifying. And a much warmer world will be upon us before we know it.

GOING GREEN

In one way or another, every person on the planet contributes to global warming. And every person needs to help reduce greenhouse gas emissions. That includes YOU!

Take action! Just thinking about global warming may make you feel helpless. But you're not. You can help stop global warming. And you can start today.

Begin with a few easy steps:

- **Switch out incandescent lightbulbs in your home for energy-efficient CFLs.** Start with the lights that are on most often.

- **Don't waste paper.** Recycle it when you're done using it. Use recycled paper made from 100 percent postconsumer waste. (Check the package.)

- **Save even more paper by reading newspapers and magazines online.** Don't print them out.

- **Take showers instead of baths.**

- **Wash your clothes in cold water instead of hot or warm water.** Then dry them on a clothesline instead of in the dryer.

- **Turn off lights whenever you're not using them.**

58

Blocks of crushed aluminum cans lie in stacks, ready to be recycled.

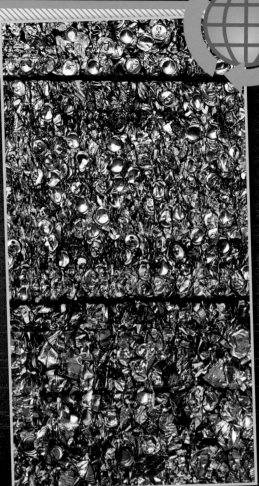

• Plug electronic devices that have a standby mode (such as computers and DVD players) into a power strip. Then turn the strip off when you're not using those devices.

Those weren't too tough, were they? You're ready to move on to a few lifestyle changes. Try some of these:

• Recycle everything you can, from cardboard and cans to plastics.

• If your school doesn't have a recycling program, start one.

• Consume less. Everything you buy has been made using energy. See if you can get a recycled version of the things you need. Try shopping at thrift stores or garage sales. You'll help the planet and save money too.

• Buy things that last so you won't have to replace them for a long time.

GOING GREEN

- **Whenever you can, walk instead of riding in a car.** If you can't walk, ride a bike. If you can't ride a bike, take public transportation.

- **Take a reusable bag or tote with you to the grocery store or on any shopping trip.** All those plastic bags are made from fossil fuels. Paper bags are made from trees.

OK, you're on a roll! Here are a few more things you can do that will help a lot to combat global warming:

- **Buy food and other things that are grown or made locally.** Encourage your parents to do this too. Most items in stores come from thousands of miles away. A lot of fossil fuel is burned to get them to your town.

- **Encourage your school or church to reduce emissions.** Start a campaign to raise money for more efficient or Earth-friendly appliances, like a new water heater or solar panels for the roof!

- Calculate your carbon footprint. Several websites, such as the U.S. Environmental Protection Agency (www.epa.gov/climatechange/emissions/ind_calculator.html), can help you do this. Take the time to figure out how you can make your footprint smaller. Then do it.

- Learn more about climate change. Stay informed of what scientists are researching and finding. Tell others what you know about global warming. Encourage them to make Earth-friendly changes too.

Make your voice heard. Write or e-mail your mayor, city council representative, or state legislator. Your letter doesn't have to be long or complicated. Not sure what to write? Here are a few lines that will help you get started.

Dear _____,

Earth is warming because things people are doing are adding too many greenhouse gases to the air. Global warming is changing the planet. It's affecting plants, animals, and people. I'm concerned about global warming, and I need your help in trying to stop it. Conserving energy cuts down on greenhouse gases. I think we could conserve energy by _____.

Thanks. Earth is depending on us.
Sincerely,

_____ Age _____

GOING GREEN

Get involved! Many organizations are working to combat global warming and climate change. Here are just a few you can easily contact:

- **The Alliance to Save Energy**
  http://www.ase.org/
  1850 M Street NW, Suite 600
  Washington, DC 20036
  202-857-0666

62

- **The Environmental Defense Fund**
  http://www.edf.org/home.cfm
  257 Park Avenue South
  New York, NY 10010
  800-684-3322

- **Natural Resources Defense Council**
  http://www.nrdc.org
  40 West 20th Street
  New York, NY 10011
  212-727-2700

• **Sierra Club**
http://www.sierraclub.org
National Headquarters
85 Second Street, 2nd Floor
San Francisco, CA 94105
415-977-5500

Every person can make a difference. That's because small, positive changes do matter. And small, positive changes multiplied millions of times (tell your friends!) produce immense benefits that can truly change the world.

GLOSSARY

atmosphere: the layer of gases that surrounds Earth

biomass: plants or plant waste materials that can be used to generate heat or electricity

carbon credit: a credit that a person, company, or country can buy to offset carbon dioxide or other greenhouse gas emissions

carbon cycle: the cyclical process by which carbon moves through the natural world

carbon dioxide (CO_2): an odorless, colorless gas that is a mix of carbon and oxygen; the primary greenhouse gas

carbon footprint: a measure of how much carbon dioxide an individual, group, company, or country produces

carbon neutral: taking in and releasing the same amount of carbon. Biomass is a carbon-neutral power source. People can offset their carbon footprint to become carbon neutral.

climate: usual weather patterns, or the typical weather in a specific region

climate change: a change in normal climate patterns

climate model: a computer model that analyzes climate data to make projections about how climate may change due to global warming

deforestation: the removal of all the trees in an area, usually by cutting or burning

emissions: something sent forth, or released. Released gases that contribute to global warming are called emissions.

evaporation: the process of changing from a liquid into a gas

fossil fuel: a fuel such as oil, coal, and natural gas that formed underground from plants and animals that died millions of years ago

glacier: a large mass of ice in mountain regions that is moving slowly downhill

global warming: the recent warming of Earth's surface and the air just above it, caused by increased carbon dioxide and other heat-trapping gases in the atmosphere. The theory of global warming has been supported by most scientific study.

greenhouse effect: the natural process by which heat is temporarily trapped by the atmosphere rather than radiating directly out into space

greenhouse gas: a name for carbon dioxide and other polluting gases that hold the sun's heat near Earth. These gases cause the greenhouse effect.

ice core: a long cylinder of ice extracted from glaciers and ice sheets

ice sheet: a vast expanse of immensely thick ice on land

ice shelf: part of an ice sheet that extends from land onto water

methane: an odorless, colorless gas; much natural methane is produced by bacteria when dead materials decay; a greenhouse gas

nitrous oxide: a colorless, slightly sweet-smelling gas. Nitrous oxide is a greenhouse gas.

permafrost: permanently frozen soil

photosynthesis: the process by which plants use energy from the sun to convert carbon dioxide and water into sugar and oxygen

photovoltaic: able to generate an electric current when exposed to light

sea level rise: an increase in the average level of the oceans worldwide

solar energy: energy from the sun

sustainable: practiced or used in a way that doesn't destroy or permanently damage a resource

visible light: part of solar energy that human eyes can see

water vapor: a gas that forms when liquid water evaporates

SELECTED BIBLIOGRAPHY

Blackwell Publishing. "North American Birds Moving North as a Result of Climate Change." *ScienceDaily.* June 14, 2007. http://www.sciencedaily.com/releases/2007/06/070611112536.htm (November 9, 2007).

Brahic, Catherine. "Blame for Global Warming Placed Firmly on Humankind." *New Scientist Environment.* February 5, 2007. http://environment.newscientist.com/channel/earth/dn11088-blame-for-global-warming-placed-firmly-on humankind.html (February 13, 2007).

British Broadcasting Corporation. "Climate Changes Shift Springtime." *BBC News.* August 25, 2006. http://news.bbc.co.uk/2/hi/science/nature/5279390.stm (August 27, 2006).

——. "Climate Scepticism: The Top 10." *BBC News.* November 12, 2007. http://news.bbc.co.uk/2/hi/in_depth/629/629/7074601.stm (December 11, 2007).

Conservation International. "Climate Change May Threaten More Than One Million Species with Extinction." *ScienceDaily.* January 8, 2004. http://www.sciencedaily.com/releases/2004/01/040108080103.htm (January 6, 2008).

Coorey, Madeleine. "Australian Drought Linked to Global Warming." *TerraDaily.* April 20, 2007. http://www.terradaily.com/reports/Australian_Drought_Linked_To_Global_Warming_999.html (April 30, 2007).

Dessler, Andrew E., and Edward A. Parson. *The Science and Politics of Global Climate Change.* New York: Cambridge University Press, 2006.

Dow, Kirstin, and Thomas E. Downing. *The Atlas of Climate Change: Mapping the World's Greatest Challenge.* Berkeley: University of California Press, 2007.

Gore, Al. *An Inconvenient Truth: The Planetary Emergency of Global Warming and What We Can Do about It.* Emmaus, PA: Rodale, 2006.

Harrabin, Roger. "China 'Now Top Carbon Polluter'" *BBC News.* April 14, 2008. http://news.bbc.co.uk/2/hi/asia-pacific/7347638.stm (April 14, 2008).

Intergovernmental Panel on Climate Change. "Fourth Assessment Report: Climate Change 2007." *IPCC Reports.* 2007. http://www.ipcc.ch/ipccreports/assessments-reports.htm (February 18, 2008).

Met Office Hadley Centre. "Climate Change and the Greenhouse Effect: A Briefing from the Hadley Centre." *Met Office Hadley Centre Brochures.* December 2005. http://www.metoffice.gov.uk/research/hadleycentre/pubs/brochures/2005/climate_greenhouse.pdf (February 18, 2008).

National Aeronautics and Space Administration. "The Roles of the Ocean in Climate Change." *NASA: About the Terra Spacecraft.* N.d. http://terra.nasa.gov/FactSheets/Oceans (April 16, 2007).

National Snow and Ice Data Center. "Arctic Sea Ice Shrinks as Temperatures Rise." *NSIDC Press Room.* October 3, 2006. http://nsidc.org/news/press/2006_seaiceminimum/20061003_pressrelease.html (December 28, 2006).

Pew Center on Global Climate Change. "Climate Change 101: International Action." *Pew Center on Global Climate Change: Global Warming Basics.* 2006. http://www.pewclimate.org/docUploads/PEW_Climate%20101%20Intl.pdf (July 7, 2007).

Roach, John. "Arctic Melt Opens Northwest Passage." *National Geographic News.* September 17, 2007. http://news.nationalgeographic.com/news/pf/38614724.html (April 5, 2008).

TerraNature Trust. "Melting Permafrost Methane Emissions: The Other Threat to Climate Change." *TerraNature.* September 15, 2006. http://www.terranature.org/methaneSiberia.htm (December 5, 2007).

Weart, Spencer. "The Discovery of Global Warming." *Center for History of Physics: Online Exhibits.* August 2007. http://www.aip.org/history/climate (August 18, 2007).

World Meteorological Organization. "Top 11 Warmest Years on Record Have All Been in Last 13 Years. *Science Daily.* December 13, 2007. http://www.sciencedaily.com/releases/2007/12/071213101419.htm (April 10, 2008).

FURTHER READING

BOOKS

Cherry, Lynne, and Gary Braasch. *How We Know What We Know about Our Changing Climate*. Nevada City, CA: Dawn Publications, 2008. This book reveals how young people have been involved in research projects that support climate scientists and how readers can do their own research.

David, Laurie, and Cambria Gordon. *The Down-to-Earth Guide to Global Warming*. New York: Orchard Books, 2007. The *Down-to-Earth Guide* is a lighthearted look at global warming and what can be done about it.

Gore, Al. *An Inconvenient Truth: the Crisis of Global Warming*. New York: Viking Children's Books, 2007. Based on former Vice President Al Gore's best-selling book about global warming and climate change, this well-illustrated overview of global warming is appropriate for young adult readers.

Maslin, Mark. *Global Warming: Causes, Effects, and the Future*. St. Paul, MN: Voyageur Press, 2007. Mark Maslin is a climate scientist at University College London in the United Kingdom. He has written extensively about global warming and climate change in books and magazines and for television.

Revkin, Andrew. *The North Pole Was Here: Puzzles and Perils at the Top of the World*. Kingfisher: 2006. This exciting book relates environmental reporter Andrew Revkin's trip to the North Pole, where he worked with a research team studying the relationship between disappearing sea ice and global warming.

Thornhill, Jan. *This Is My Planet: The Kids' Guide to Global Warming*. Toronto, Ontario: Maple Tree Press, 2007. Touching on many different aspects of global warming, this lively book contains suggestions for reducing your carbon footprint, plus several experiments.

WEBSITES

Beat the Heat

http://beattheheat.nrdc.org/

Find out what other people around the country are saying about global warming.
Add your own comments to the interactive map.

Climate Connections: A Global Journey

http://www.npr.org/news/specials/climate/interactive/?ps=bb4

This interactive website created by National Public Radio lets readers see and hear
about the impacts of climate change on people in many different parts of the world.

EnergyStar

http://www.energystar.gov/index.cfm?fuseaction=popuptool.atHome

Explore an interactive house and learn dozens of ways to save energy on this
website, created by the Environmental Protection Agency and the Department of
Energy.

Lick Global Warming

http://www.lickglobalwarming.org/

Send a letter to Congress, play a global warming game, and learn ways to combat
global warming.

National Geographic Climate Connections

http://ngm.nationalgeographic.com/ngm/climateconnections

National Geographic magazine created this website, where visitors can read articles
about climate change and view pictures of its impacts worldwide.

World Wildlife Fund

http://www.panda.org/about_wwf/what_we_do/climate_change/what_you_can_
do/index.cfm

This section of the World Wildlife Fund's website gives ways to help slow global
warming and climate change. It includes an "Ecological Footprint Quiz" and a link to a
carbon footprint calculator.

69

INDEX

animals and plants, impact of global
  warming on, 38–39
Antarctica, 22, 29, 32, 33
Arctic, 4–5, 29, 31, 32, 34
atmosphere, 8–9, 10
average surface temperature, 6, 15,
  29

biodiesel, 51, 53

California, laws to limit emissions in,
  45–46
Canada, 5
carbon credits, 44, 45, 57
carbon cycle, 11–13, 20
carbon dioxide: heat-trapping power
  of, 14, 21; increase in atmospheric
  levels, 21–22; link to Earth's surface
  temperature, 23, 29; sources of,
  10–11, 18, 20, 34
carbon footprint, 57, 61
carbon-neutral lifestyle, 56–57
carbon trading, 44, 46
cars, 16, 18, 48–49, 52
cement, production of, 19, 20
chlorofluorocarbons (CFCs), 14, 15

climate, 24, 27
climate change, 26, 39; projections
  and evidence, 29–39
climate models, 26–28
compact fluorescent lightbulbs
  (CFLs), 50, 58

droughts, 35, 37

energy conservation, 52–53
ethanol, 50–51

fires, 10, 20, 35
floods, 35, 36, 37
fossil fuels: burning of, 15, 16, 18, 19;
  formation, 13; reducing use of, 48,
  50

glaciers, 24, 26, 30–32, 33
global warming: definition, 6;
  scientific agreement about, 23, 40
greenhouse effect, 8–9, 13, 15, 23
greenhouse gases: definition,
  9; heat-trapping power of,
  14–15; types, 10, 14; ways to reduce
  emissions, 58–61

Greenland, 22, 25, 32, 33

Hansen, James, 40–41

ice cores, 22
Industrial Revolution, 18
Intergovernmental Panel on Climate
    Change (IPCC), 42, 43

Keeling, Charles David, 21
Kyoto Protocol, 43, 46

methane, 14, 34

nitrous oxide, 14

ocean temperature, 30
ozone layer, 15

permafrost, 34
photosynthesis, 11, 12, 20
polar bears, 4–5
PS10 solar power tower, 54

recycling, 53–54, 58, 59
renewable energy, 54–56
Russia, 5

sea ice, 4–5, 30–31, 32
sea level, 26, 33
seasonal change, 37–38
severe weather, 35–37
solar energy, 6–9, 23, 55

tundra, 34

United Nations Framework
    Convention on Climate Change
    (UNFCCC), 42–43
U.S. Mayors Climate Protection
    Agreement, 46

water vapor, 10, 14

71

ABOUT THE AUTHOR

Rebecca L. Johnson is the author of many award-winning books for children and young adults on a wide variety of science topics. She first wrote about global warming and climate change in the 1990s, in her book *The Greenhouse Effect: Life on a Warmer Planet*. More recently, Johnson worked with an international team of climate scientists from the Committee on Earth Observation Satellites (CEOS). They prepared a report outlining the key role of satellites in gathering information about global warming and climate change. The report was presented at UNFCCC climate meetings in Nairobi, Kenya, in late 2006. Johnson lives in Sioux Falls, South Dakota.

PHOTO ACKNOWLEDGMENTS

The images in this book are used with the permission of: NASA , pp. 1 (inset), 3 (top inset), 4-5 (main); © Bill Hauser/Independent Picture Service, pp. 1 (background top right), 3 (background), 9, 12, 26; © iStockphoto. com/MaxFX, p. 1 (background main); © Robert Mann/SuperStock, p. 3 (bottom inset); NASA/GSFC, pp. 4 (inset), 31 (both); © age fotostock/SuperStock, pp. 5, 16, 17; © iStockphoto.com, p. 6; © Maremagnum/ Photographer's Choice/Getty Images, p. 7; U.S. Fish and Wildlife Service, p. 10; © David Wrobel/Visuals Unlimited, p. 11 (bottom); © iStockphoto.com/Stephen Sweet, p. 11 (top); NASA/JPL, p. 13; Agricultural Research Service, USDA, p. 14; © iStockphoto.com/Nick Schlax, p. 15; © Jacques Jangoux/Alamy, p. 20; Scripps Institution of Oceanography/UC San Diego, p. 21; © Vin Morgan/AFP/Getty Images, p. 22; © Roger Braithwaite/Peter Arnold, Inc., p. 24; © WorldFoto/Alamy, p. 25; © Scientifica/Visuals Unlimited, p. 27; © Biosphoto/Vernay Pierre/Peter Arnold, Inc., p. 29; Japan Coast Guard/Argo Information Centre, http:// argo.jcommops.org, p. 30; © iStockphoto.com/Rafael Ramirez Lee, p. 32; © Gary Braasch, p. 34; © William West/AFP/Getty Images, p. 35; © Arif Ali/AFP/Getty Images, p. 36; © Gilles Mingasson/Getty Images, p. 38; © Jordin Althaus/WireImage/Getty Images, p. 40; © Jorg Greuel/Digital Vision/Getty Images, p. 41; AP Photo/Eduardo DiBaia, p. 42; AP Photo/Fernando Bustamante, p. 43; © iStockphoto.com/Julie Ridge, p. 45 (top); AP Photo/Ben Margot, p. 45 (bottom); © China Photos/Getty Images, p. 47; AP Photo/ Yuri Kageyama, p. 48; © Todd Bigelow/Aurora/Getty Images, p. 49; © Todd Strand/Independent Picture Service, pp. 50, 52; © Karen Bleier/AFP/Getty Images, p. 51; © Photodisc/Getty Images, pp. 53, 59; © Denis Doyle/Getty Images, p. 54; © Justin Sullivan/Getty Images, p. 55; © Sean Gallup/Getty Images, p. 56.

Cover: © Berndt-Joel Gunnarsson/Nordic Photos/Getty Images, (top left); NASA (top right); NASA/ JSC (bottom right); © iStockphoto.com/MaxFX (background main, type and spine); © Bill Hauser/ Independent Picture Service (background top right).